A Brilliant Streak

THE MAKING OF MARK TWAIN

by Kathryn Lasky

Illustrated by Barry Moser

HARCOURT BRACE & COMPANY

San Diego · New York · London

Library of Congress Cataloging-in-Publication Data
Lasky, Kathryn.
A brilliant streak: the making of Mark Twain/by Kathryn Lasky;
illustrated by Barry Moser.
p.   cm.
Summary: An illustrated biography of young Samuel Clemens,
who grew up to be the writer known as Mark Twain.
ISBN 0-15-252110-0
1. Twain, Mark, 1835–1910—Biography—Juvenile literature.   2. Authors,
American—19th century—Biography—Juvenile literature.   [1. Twain, Mark,
1835–1910.   2. Authors, American.]   I. Moser, Barry, ill.   II. Title.
PS1331.L37   1998
818'.409—dc20
[B]   95-18479

First edition   F E D C B A

Printed in Singapore

A BRILLIANT STREAK

I was born excited

I was born the 30th of November, 1835, in the almost invisible village of Florida, Monroe County, Missouri. The village contained a hundred people and I increased the population by 1 percent. It is more than many of the best men in history could have done for a town. . . . There is no record of a person doing as much—not even Shakespeare. —from *MARK TWAIN'S AUTOBIOGRAPHY*

ONE autumn night more than a hundred and sixty years ago, a comet streaked across the sky over the tiny village of Florida, Missouri. That same night, in a clapboard cabin, Jane Lampton Clemens gave birth to her sixth child—Samuel Langhorne Clemens. He was premature and feeble. Jane and her husband, John, did not expect the baby to survive.

The comet left a luminous glow long after it passed. Looking out the window, Jane Clemens might have felt that the comet was a sign, that there must be a link between the glorious fire in the sky and the tiny wrinkled baby she held in her arms on Earth.

His parents hoped that Samuel would live through the night. He did. In fact, he lived until Halley's comet returned seventy-five years later. And between those two brilliant streaks in the sky, Samuel Langhorne Clemens lived enough lives for half a dozen other people as well.

But there were many close calls. More than once—because of a combination of frail health and a mischievous nature—Sam had a close shave with death. If it wasn't measles or pneumonia, it was near-drownings. It is rumored that his parents became so used to sitting by his bed, waiting for him to die, they often fell asleep during the ordeal.

Even when Sam was safe from real dangers like illnesses and drownings, he tormented himself with imaginary ones—Indian massacres, hangings, and robberies. Sam could construct the most terrifying pictures of these tragedies, and as a child his nightmares were so fierce that he often walked in his sleep. His uncle once found him in a trance, in the middle of the night, sitting on top of a horse in the barn; he had walked there during a particularly horrid dream. Sam could vividly imagine any experience he heard about, and sometimes it was too much for him. "I was born excited," Sam wrote later, explaining that as a child he could remember everything, whether it had actually happened or not.

Sam's excited imagination led him to become a truth stretcher, a manipulator of facts, and on occasion an outright liar. He was the first to admit it, claiming that although he couldn't remember his first lie, he told his second when he was nine days old and pretended that a diaper pin was sticking him. He said that at six weeks of age he helped his grandfather drink a toddy of whiskey. And he told his friends that his younger brother, Henry, had walked into a fire when he was just one week old! Sam never told lies to hurt anybody. His chief aim in telling a lie was to impress people—to make himself look funnier, braver, more daring than he really was—but never to make another person appear a fool.

The combination, however, of stretching the truth, lying, and "remembering" things that might not have happened made Samuel Clemens into one of the greatest storytellers ever—the man the world knows as Mark Twain.

When Sam was four years old, his father, John Marshall Clemens, became worried about money and moved his family across the river to Hannibal, Missouri, where he opened a law practice and a small general store. He eventually became Judge Clemens, a justice of the peace. Hannibal was Sam's home for the next thirteen years.

As Sam grew older he showed no signs of curbing his imagination or losing his fascination with danger. He had to be watched constantly or he would run down to the river to "swim" and nearly drown. His mother, desperate for a little peace, sent him to school when he was four and a half. He hated it. There were rules, there were schoolbooks, and there were prayers. He broke the rules and he was bored by the schoolbooks. But much to his delight, when he prayed for gingerbread one day, he got it. A little girl near him forgot to hide her piece from his watchful eyes, and he quickly snatched it away. Sam was impressed by the power of prayer and for the next several days prayed frequently, but there was no more gingerbread.

3

Once, when the teacher was angry with Sam for breaking a rule, she sent him out to cut a switch so she could whip him. He came back with a wood shaving two inches wide and less than an eighth of an inch thick. She promptly sent another boy to cut a bigger switch.

School did not improve, and as Sam grew older, he became better at finding ways to escape the classroom. Before getting up in the morning, he would check himself over for any little rash, bump, or bruise that might keep him home. If he was lucky and found something, he would begin

groaning immediately. He'd had a lot of practice during his real childhood illnesses. But he was no longer so frail, and acting sick became harder. He often played hooky, particularly on those days when the air was warm, the sun was bright, and the river was calling. There were fish to catch, caves to explore, and, of course, the Mississippi to swim in.

To make sure he hadn't played hooky and gone swimming on warm spring mornings, his mother would sew a thread attaching both sides of his collar and then check it when he returned from school. His favorite place was Bear Creek, because you could swim naked there. They had rules about swimming naked in Hannibal.

In the winter, when patches of the river froze, Sam and his friends were drawn there to go skating, preferably at night and without permission. For Sam there was no fun in doing something with permission. Once, when Sam and his friend Tom Nash were skimming along the ice on a moonlit night, they heard a dark rumbling. The ice was breaking up; they were a half mile from shore. The clouds rolled in and it became difficult to see where the ice was solid. The boys raced for the shore, dodging patches of open water between the dwindling ice blocks and springing from cake to cake. When they were near shore, Tom fell through. He did not drown but came down with a fever that left him completely deaf.

Yet nothing discouraged the boys from such adventures; the forbidden was always attractive.

Another friend, Tom Blankenship, son of the town drunkard, was not considered suitable company for Christian children and was therefore especially interesting. Tom was, according to Sam, "ignorant, unwashed, insufficiently fed; but he had as good a heart as ever any boy had. . . . He was the only really independent person—boy or man—in the community, and by consequence he was . . . continuously happy, and was envied by all the rest of us." Tom Blankenship became the model for the most famous character Mark Twain would ever create—Huckleberry Finn. Not completely forbidden, but almost as irresistible as the river and the friendship of Tom Blankenship, was McDowell's Cave, a vast limestone cavern owned by an odd man: Dr. McDowell, a St. Louis surgeon, who at one time stored in it guns and ammunition for an invasion of Mexico. When Sam first went there, he and Tom Blankenship took a stolen skiff, painted it red, fitted it with a sail, and sailed it down the river to the cave. The cave ran for miles and was "a tangled wilderness of narrow and lofty clefts . . . [and] passages" and secret chambers. It was scary, and Sam could imagine the spirits of ghosts in the wavering light of the candle he carried. There were as many rumors about the place as there were pathways through it. It was said that several people had become lost in the cave and had died there. A cylinder in one of the most hidden and secret places in the cave contained the perfectly preserved corpse of a young girl, said to be the owner's daughter. Sam found a strange and intense pleasure in this terror, and the cave soon became one of his favorite haunts. There were lovely, silky little bats that Sam often caught to bring home to his mother, as well as snakes.

Sam never forgot the delicious terror of the first visit, and he would relive it when he wrote about Tom Sawyer and Becky Thatcher becoming lost for three days in the cave in *The Adventures of Tom Sawyer*. For young Sam it was a place where he and his friends played whenever they could. In addition to housing corpses, bats, and hidden passageways, the cave seemed like a perfect place to find pirates' gold. And as Sam later wrote in *Tom Sawyer*, "There comes a time in every rightly constructed boy's life when he has a raging desire to go somewhere and dig for treasure."

Being a treasure hunter, heading up a band of robbers, joining a circus, and becoming a pirate were all ambitions that threaded through Sam's boyhood.

He and his comrades, however, shared one permanent ambition—to become steamboatmen on the longest river in America, the Mississippi.

"Once a day a cheap, gaudy packet arrived upward from St. Louis, and another downward from Keokuk. Before these events, the day was glorious with expectancy; after them, the day was a dead and empty thing," Sam would write in his account of growing up on the river.

Sam knew that you could not become a steamboat pilot right off. His first dream, therefore, was to be a cabin boy so that he could come out on deck wearing a white apron and shake a tablecloth over the side of the boat, where all his old friends could see him. He and his buddies were consumed with jealousy when one boy from the village was hired on as an apprentice. When the boy's boat pulled into Hannibal, the young man would make great displays of scrubbing a rusty bolt. Or he would strut about the wharf in his blackest, greasiest clothes "so nobody would forget that he was a steamboatman." He talked about "St. Looey" like an old citizen, to Sam and his friends' great irritation. In Sam's eyes this boy had everything—"hair oil, money, and a silver watch on a showy brass watch chain." Sam and every one of his friends admired the cabin boy and hated him at the same time, and their dreams of becoming steamboatmen grew fiercer than ever. For Sam the realization of the dream was a long time coming.

In many of Mark Twain's books people die by drowning. This was an area of expertise for Sam, who by the age of nine was almost drowning on a regular basis. Expertise was essential to Mark Twain, who always tried to write what he knew—whether or not it had actually happened. He might tell lies, but they were honest lies and had a certain unvarnished truth about them. He was, despite the lies, interested in truth—though not necessarily in accuracy. "A man's private thoughts," he once said, "can never be a lie; what he thinks, is to him the truth, always." In Samuel Clemens's mind, he had drowned at least eight times, almost once a year, by the time he was nine years old. And that to him was the truth!

Along with many of his friends, Sam took up smoking a corncob pipe when he was nine, but he soon preferred cigars. He also took up swearing. All in private.

He knew his mother would be more upset by the swearing than the smoking; back then no one knew how dangerous smoking is to a person's health, but swearing was certainly not good for a Christian soul.

Sam's mother tried very hard to give her son proper religious training. She worried about his endangered soul as much as she once had about his frail body. But even the vivid pictures of hell painted by the preachers from

the pulpit of the Methodist church could not compare in excitement to the escapades of robbers, pirates, and massacring Indian warriors. To make church a little more exciting, Sam and a friend once sneaked a deck of cards into the service and dared to play a hidden game of euchre in the vestry. After nearly getting caught, they slipped the cards into the sleeves of the preacher's baptismal robes, which were hanging in a closet. A short time later, when the preacher was baptizing a new convert in the river, the cards floated up. To Sam's delight he saw three aces bobbing on the surface of the water.

Sometimes Sam was tempted by religion, though, especially if it involved dressing up. Sam joined the church-sponsored Cadets of Temperance and actually gave up smoking. If he pledged not to smoke or swear, he could wear a red merino sash and march in the May Day and Fourth of July parades. Sam lasted three months—getting to wear a sash just twice a year was not enough incentive to give up bad words and tobacco. He never regretted giving things up for short periods of time, however, because when he returned to his bad habits he took even more pleasure in them.

Except for the prayer that brought him gingerbread when he was four years old, Sam had little use for organized religion and thought Christianity and all other religions were a pack of "lies and swindles."

For Sam the lies of religion were not good yarns and could never compare to his own kinds of lies and stretchings of the truth. In Sam's mind, religion only made people feel bad.

Indeed, Sam's fondest memory of religious training was the crooked fingernail of his Sunday school teacher Mr. Richmond; it twisted and curved to a point, like a parrot's beak. He was genuinely fond of Mr. Richmond, who never seemed to notice that Sam always repeated the same five Bible verses to win his prizes. Over the years that he was in Richmond's class, Sam collected several "dreary books," books that had only good boys in them.

After the Clemenses moved to Hannibal, Sam spent several weeks each year during summer vacation at his aunt and uncle's farm near Florida. These weeks were his salvation from the rigors of school and book learning. The farm was a "heavenly place." There were eight cousins and the food was the greatest, with ripe watermelons, fresh berries, and sweet milk, or clabber, as it was called. "I know how the wild blackberries looked, and how they tasted, and the same with the paw-paws. . . . I can feel the thumping rain, upon my head, of hickory nuts and walnuts when we were out in the frosty dawn to scramble for them with the pigs. . . . I know the stain of blackberries, and how pretty it is. . . . I know how a prize watermelon looks when it is sunning its fat rotundity."

There were plenty of places on the farm to almost drown in, and best of all there were wonderful ghost stories to hear from Uncle Dan'l, a slave. Sam and his cousins and the slave children would gather in Uncle Dan'l's cabin in the evening and sit around the hearth with the firelight playing across their faces. Sam, who was as good a listener as he was a storyteller, would remember for the rest of his life the "creepy joy" that quivered through him when Uncle Dan'l told ghost stories.

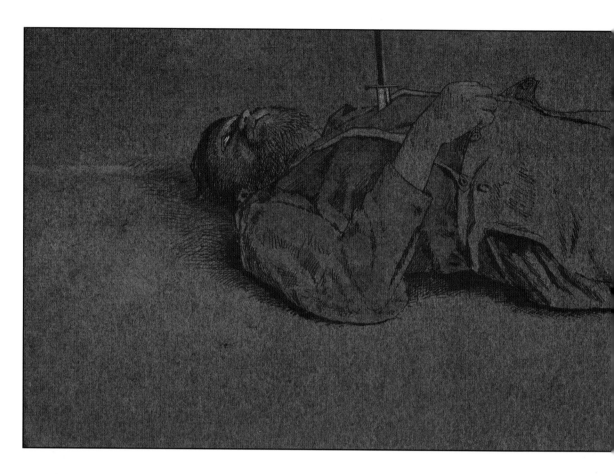

When Sam was eight years old, a murder occurred in Hannibal. Two drunk farmers got into a fight that ended in the stabbing of one of them. It happened on a day when Sam had played hooky. He was afraid to return home after dark because he knew he would get thrashed. So he decided to postpone his return by climbing through the window of his father's office to nap on the couch. As he lay there he fancied he could see a "long, dusky, shapeless thing stretched on the floor. A cold shiver ran through me. . . ." Frightened, he turned his back to it, but soon the suspense got the better of him. He turned over once more and in a shaft of moonlight saw a pale face with its eyes "fixed and glassy in death."

It was McFarland, the farmer who had been murdered. The knife was in his chest, and although he had been dead for hours, it appeared to Sam as if the wound still bled. The man had been carried in to Judge Clemens's office to be doctored. The image of the bleeding stab wound haunted Sam for a long time, and many years later, in *The Innocents Abroad*, he wrote of that terrible night tinged with blood and moonlight.

Barely a year later, Sam was quietly sitting on the fence outside his house, whittling, when a man pulled out a gun and shot an old man named Sam Smarr, who had been drunk and insulted him the week before. The townsfolk carried Smarr into the drugstore, and Sam followed.

"Get back! Give him some air!" someone called, but then, according to Sam, some "thoughtful idiot" placed a huge Bible on the dying man's chest. Sam, who was standing nearby, never got over the torturous image of that Bible rising and falling on the man's chest as he struggled to breathe. For Sam the experience was yet another reason to distance himself from religion.

This incident was not the end of the violence that Sam witnessed as a child. On a fishing expedition with friends, he came upon the body of a runaway slave who had drowned in the river. And in the streets of Hannibal, a very young Sam saw an abolitionist attacked by a mob of people ready to lynch him. Another time he saw the dreadful slave trader William Beebe with his human cargo of slaves chained together, waiting to be shipped downriver to New Orleans.

To be shipped downriver was the worst fate a Missouri slave could endure. The brutal plantation work of the Deep South shortened a slave's life by several years. The people of Hannibal never doubted the institution of slavery, but they did feel compassion for the slaves sent downriver.

The sad faces of the slaves stirred a misery in Sam that he would never forget. But he did not know slavery was wrong. His own family owned slaves. The Bible condoned slavery, and preachers did, too.

The first time that Sam ever questioned the institution of slavery was when he grumbled to his mother about a little slave boy named Sandy, who sang and whooped and hollered all day long. The noise annoyed Sam.

When he complained, Jane Clemens's eyes filled with tears. "Poor thing," she said, "when he sings it shows he is not remembering, and that comforts me." What the child was not remembering was being separated from his mother when they were both sold to different owners. Sam never complained to his mother again about Sandy and from that day on began to seriously question the ownership of one human being by another.

Sam learned more outside the classroom than in it. He learned about greed and murder. He learned how to listen to some of the best storytellers in the land. He learned about the beauty of a blackberry stain and how to tell if a melon was ready to eat. And he learned about the tragedy of slavery.

Uncle Dan'l became Jim, the runaway slave who belonged to the Widow Douglas and with whom Huckleberry Finn begins his river journey. All through *Adventures of Huckleberry Finn*, Huck wrestles with the notion that he is helping a fugitive slave, depriving the widow of her rightful property. The law of the land says he must return Jim to the widow. Huck fears that not only the law will get after him but the Lord, too, for stealing a slave: "My wickedness was being watched all the time from up there in heaven. . . . I was trying to say I would do the right thing and go and write to owner and tell where he was, but deep down in me I knowed it was a lie. . . . You can't pray a lie."

Samuel Clemens learned what the Bible and the Methodist ministers could not teach him—that slavery was wrong and that you cannot pray lies. When Sam grew up and became the writer Mark Twain, he had Huck say it for him.

To be a steamboatman

I loved the profession far better than any I have followed since. . . . The reason is plain: A pilot, in those days, was the only unfettered and entirely independent human being that lived on earth. Kings are but the hampered servants of parliament. . . . In truth, every man, woman, and child has a master, but . . . the Mississippi pilot had none.
—from *LIFE ON THE MISSISSIPPI*

WHEN Sam was eleven his father died, and very shortly after that his schooldays stopped. The family simply did not have enough money and Sam had to go to work. Sam's first job was that of a printer's apprentice, or as it was called, a printer's devil, in the office of the *Hannibal Courier*.

He lived in the home of a Mr. Joseph Ament and was to be given food and board and two new suits of clothes a year. But Ament was a stingy soul, and Sam only got one new suit of clothing; the other was a hand-me-down from Ament, who was considerably bigger. The food was so sparse that Sam often slipped down to the cellar to snitch an onion or a raw potato.

His tasks as a printer's devil were to set type accurately, wash up the type forms in which the type is composed, distribute type back in the cases, and run the job press. He was also in charge of circulation, which meant he delivered the papers. The most interesting part of the job was minding the telegraph wire during the last year of the Mexican War. The recently invented telegraph carried the news across the Mississippi to Hannibal, and Sam was given the job of editing the news off the wire from the battlefield. He saw history and literature in the making.

When Sam had completed his two years of apprenticeship at the *Courier,* his brother Orion bought a newspaper, the *Hannibal Journal,* for five hundred dollars. Sam immediately went to work for him, and their younger

brother, Henry, just twelve, was also taken out of school to learn typesetting. In an attempt to increase circulation when Orion was out of town, Sam tried to spice up the paper with local news, humor, gossip, and sensationalism. He exposed a fraud who was charging admission to see a panorama of Napoleon Bonaparte crossing the Rhine; the spectacle actually consisted of a broken bone on a piece of bacon rind. He reported that the editor of a rival newspaper was so heartsick over a broken love affair that he had gone upriver to drown himself. Sam gave a vivid account and even engraved illustrations showing the editor wading out to test the depths with a stick. Circulation did pick up, but when Orion returned he was furious. There was no more of this kind of local news, and the paper eventually failed.

After five years of hard labor, Sam had mastered a trade. Now, in 1853, seventeen-year-old Sam set out on his own. He went upriver to St. Louis, where he earned enough money in the composing room of the *Evening News* to get to New York and then Philadelphia, where he worked on two more newspapers. Finally he settled in Keokuk, Iowa, where Orion lived with his new bride. Once more Sam worked for Orion in a printing office that Orion had started. This business was as shaky as the newspaper had been. And Orion, because he could not afford to pay Sam much, made him a partner.

One bitterly cold day when Sam was walking down Main Street, a slip of paper blew into his path. When he leaned down to pick it up, he saw it was a fifty-dollar bill! For several months Sam had dreamed of going to explore the Amazon, which had recently been surveyed and written about widely. Sam had no idea in practical terms how long a journey it would be. But with the fifty-dollar bill he felt he could at least make a start.

The start took him as far as Cincinnati, Ohio, where he worked as a printer for another newspaper until the following spring, in 1857. Then he was ready for the next leg of the trip to the Amazon. He packed his valise and boarded an ancient tub called the *Paul Jones,* headed for New Orleans. But as he traveled down the Mississippi, an older dream began to smolder around the edges of the Amazon dream—that of becoming a steamboatman.

On the trip to New Orleans, he made a point of never wearing a hat so he could acquire the weather-beaten look of a river man. With great joy he greeted the first tiny blisters on his nose. By Louisville, Sam was perfecting his skill of striking casual poses against the rail. Such postures, he felt, suggested that indeed he was a genuine part of the steamboat's family. He would wait eagerly to attract the attention of the big blustery mate, and when the mate roared a general order for a capstan bar to be brought, Sam sprang to it "like a ragpicker asked to serve a monarch." Sam's longtime ambition of being a steamboatman returned full force. He forgot all about the Amazon and set himself to the task of learning the great Mississippi.

He quickly negotiated a deal with Horace Bixby, a pilot of the *Paul Jones*. For five hundred dollars, Bixby would teach him the river between New Orleans and St. Louis.

"What is the shape of Walnut Bend?" Bixby asked Sam one day.

"He might as well have asked me my grandmother's opinion of protoplasm," Sam later wrote in *Life on the Mississippi*.

Then Bixby said, "My boy, you've got to learn the *shape* of the river perfectly. It is all there is left to steer by on a very dark night. . . ."

Sam knew he must learn the river by heart. He must carry the shape of the river in his head and know every point, bend, bar, island, and reach. He kept a notebook and wrote down page after page of notes. He learned to recognize the meaning of every wrinkle and curl of the water. A silver streak meant a new snag, a slick meant dangerous shoaling, and dimpled water marked a sunken wreck.

He learned to shave an island so close as to brush the deckhouse with overhanging branches. He knew that near New Madrid the river poured in a "chocolate tide between its solid forest walls and the spot above Dubuque where the water turned olive green. . . ."

On the bow of the steamboat a leadsman would stand and measure the water depth by dropping the lead tied to the end of a line. Each six feet, or fathom, was marked on the line. The two-fathom mark, at twelve feet down the line, was the shallowest water a steamboat could navigate without danger. *Twain* was another word for two. So the call "Mark twain" from the leadsman meant that there were only twelve feet of water and the steamboat was on the edge of danger. Those two words came to have a special meaning for Samuel Clemens.

The face of the water was like a book for Sam, a wonderful, fascinating book. But as he learned to read the book, Sam found that the poetry of the river was lost, for he came to value its features for their usefulness rather than their beauty. He later wrote that before he became a pilot, he would stand and look at the river "like one bewitched. I drank it in, in a speechless rapture. The world was new to me, and I had never seen anything like this at home . . . but a day came when I began to cease from noting the glories and the charms which the moon and the sun and the twilight wrought upon the river's face. . . ." To Sam this was a steeper price to pay than the five hundred dollars he had to give to Bixby.

While Sam was still working as a cub pilot, he found a job for his brother Henry on the packet *Pennsylvania*. His brother had not been working long when a terrible accident occurred. The ship's boilers exploded, killing 150 people, including Henry. Sam always blamed himself for his younger brother's death.

Sam worked on the river as a cub and later as a captain for four years. It was about two years after he earned his certificate as a Mississippi pilot that history seemed to erupt around Sam. The Civil War broke out. The steamboats stopped running between St. Louis and New Orleans, and Sam's career as a riverboat pilot ended abruptly. He was twenty-five years old.

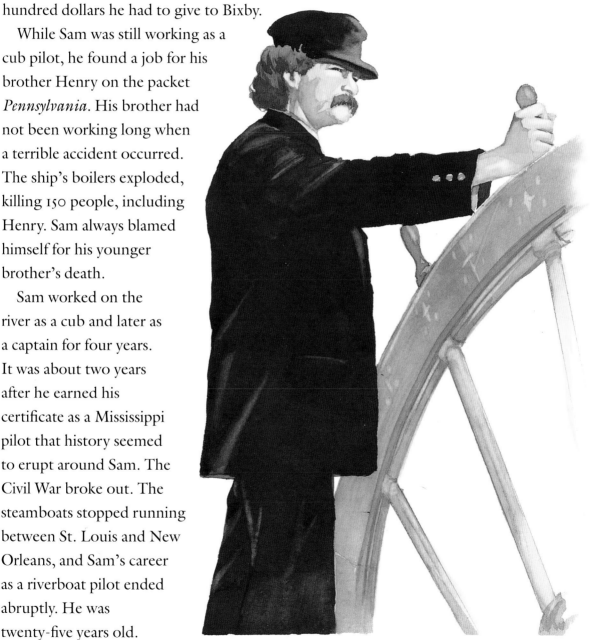

Silver fever was in the air. Sam saw and felt it as cartloads of solid silver bricks arrived daily in town. Every few days there were discoveries of new veins and new mines. The newspaper was full of stories about vagabonds becoming overnight millionaires, and it wasn't long before Sam gave up his job as secretary to the secretary and set out to hunt for silver and explore the Territory.

His first step was to buy a genuine "Mexican Plug," a horse that would be steady but docile and slow. Sam, however, was swindled. The horse was no plug. As soon as Sam got in the saddle, the animal "placed all his feet in a bunch together, lowered his back, and then suddenly arched it upward, and shot me straight into the air. . . . Pen cannot describe how I was jolted up. Imagination cannot conceive how disjointed I was—how internally, externally, and universally I was unsettled, mixed up, and ruptured." Instead of a horse, Sam realized, he had bought himself his own private earthquake.

But finally he set out with a group of friends to start prospecting. They scrambled up mountainsides, stared down rattlesnakes, scratched their way through sagebrush, and clambered over rocks and snow until they were exhausted— but they found not one speck of silver. The temptation was always there, though, for at every turn Sam met men who believed that within the next foot of an undeveloped claim fifty thousand dollars in silver would gush up like Old Faithful. They would even try to sell a few inches, or maybe as much as a foot, of rock in a claim, just so they

could buy their next meal.

At one point Sam and his friends did stake a claim, sink a shaft, and, laden with picks, crowbars, and blasting powder, begin to dig. For more than a week they toiled; all they got for their labors were pocketfuls of rocks.

Any silver that was to be found was embedded in rock and had to be milled. For a time Sam abandoned mining and figured he could make more money milling, so he went to work at a quartz mill. But finally his mining buddy Calvin Higbie talked him into trying it just one more time. This time they examined a desolate old hole that belonged to the Wide West Mining

Company. Higbie became suspicious that some of the rock coming from that shaft was not from the true vein but from an offshoot. In mining, such an offshoot is called a blind lead, for it is a lead or ledge that does not crop out above the surface. It is considered public property until it is discovered. This blind lead definitely had silver in it. All Sam and his friend had to do to make it officially theirs was to claim it and then begin work on it within the next ten days. The two young men were jubilant. At last they were millionaires.

And as Sam spun out the yarn in *Roughing It,* he claimed they were millionaires for ten whole days. But Higbie had some other important business to attend, and Sam was called to take care of a desperately ill friend. Sam left a note for Higbie explaining his absence, confident that his friend would begin to work the claim. But the note was never received. Ten days elapsed and work was not started on the blind lead. By midnight of the ninth day the word was out and miners swarmed up the hillside to take over the claim. That was just about the end of Sam's career in mining.

From Josh to Mark Twain: a writer is born

I was sired by the great American eagle and foaled by the continental dam.
   —from the *TERRITORIAL ENTERPRISE*

THIS was the opening line of a letter that poked fun at a certain public speaker's Fourth of July address in 1862. The *Territorial Enterprise* printed that letter, signed by a young man who called himself Josh. The editor of the newspaper had received Josh's letters before and enjoyed them. He found out that the true identity of Josh was Samuel Clemens and immediately wrote to him, offering a job as a local reporter for twenty-five dollars a week.

   Sam had never really thought of himself as a writer, but as he said, "Necessity is the mother of 'taking chances.'" He was ready to take this chance and declared that he was so desperate that "if . . . I had been offered a salary to translate the Talmud from the original Hebrew, I would have accepted."

   Sam hiked the 130 miles from Aurora, Nevada, to Virginia City, Nevada, in the searing summer heat. He dragged into the *Enterprise* office covered with alkali dust, his nearly waist-length red beard a tangled mess. He was awash in sweat, and clumps of hay were still sticking to him because he had slept the previous night in a hayloft. He plunked down his bedroll and

VIRGINIA CITY 130 mi.

declared, "My starboard leg seems unshipped. I'd like about one hundred yards of line; I think I'm falling to pieces."

His first assignment at the *Enterprise* was to take a bath. His next was to find a story. After one day of being a reporter, he wondered if stories might be as hard to find as silver, but at last there was one: a desperado had killed a man. Sam was ready to thank the murderer. "Sir, you are a stranger to me, but you have done me a kindness this day which I can never forget." He of course never really said that to the murderer, but he did write up the murder in great detail.

For his second story—one about some emigrants who had come through town in wagons on their way west—he stretched the truth a bit. He figured the travelers would be leaving the next day, so what they didn't know couldn't hurt them. While the emigrants had indeed passed through hostile Indian territory, Sam put those wagons through "an Indian fight" without "parallel in history."

Sam enjoyed this writing life. Virginia City was the richest city in the Territory and, according to Sam, the liveliest town in America. The great Comstock Lode ran right under it. Money was everywhere and so was action. There were brass bands, hurdy-gurdy houses, banks, hotels, theaters, inquests, riots. In his office at the *Enterprise,* Sam would sit down to write. His desk often shook and the windows rattled from blasting in the Comstock Lode hundreds of feet below him.

Sam's pilot memory from his days on the Mississippi served him well as a reporter. Just as he could recall every bank, snag, and bend of the river, he could go all over town all day long and half the night, never taking a note but remembering everything he saw. And it was his river memories that finally gave him his writing name. He dropped the rather plain name of Josh and began to sign his articles Mark Twain.

Mark Twain's imagination had no limits. If the facts for a story weren't enough, he would begin to stretch a truth and sometimes spin out an entire fantasy. Mark Twain believed that his main job as a reporter was not to bore his readers, even if it meant extending the truth beyond recognition.

The *Enterprise* itself was not concerned about the rampant imagination of its new reporter. It had never been a paper known for its accuracy or love of the factual, and the popularity of Mark Twain's columns was growing rapidly.

Mark Twain was always quick to point out an injustice or the flaws of a public official. The coroner of the town was a man whom many felt did not do his job well; worse, he was stuck-up. Mark Twain hated stuck-up people. He decided to pull a hoax on the coroner by reporting that a petrified man had been found embedded in rock and that the coroner had held an inquest even though the man had been dead three hundred years. Mark Twain

reported that the coroner had given an account of the exact posture of the man, and he took special care in describing the position of the hands in relation to the face. The pose was one in which the petrified man was actually thumbing his nose at the town. Mark Twain never expected anyone to believe such a ridiculous report, but some did. Others thought the story very funny and the article was reprinted across the country. The coroner was not amused.

More pranks followed, along with more droll stories, more ridiculous hoaxes. Finally one backfired, and people became angry. Mark Twain had reported that a ladies' charitable organization that was formed to roll bandages for the Civil War and raise money for wounded veterans was in fact raising money to promote marriages between the races. This was one of the most shocking things anyone could have thought, let alone written about, in the year 1864. Mark Twain decided he had better get out of town. He took a stagecoach to San Francisco.

He began working next as a reporter for the *Morning Call*. Mark Twain saw a lot of things in San Francisco that got his dander up. He did not have to stretch the truth to say the Chinese people in San Francisco were abused, and after he saw one stoned by a gang of white bullies he wrote an article. But the *Morning Call* refused to publish it.

Mark Twain also wrote about bad politicians and corrupt policemen. His residency in San Francisco ended abruptly—once more he angered so many people, he had to flee.

He found his way into the Sacramento Valley and back into mining country, to a place called Jackass Hill. The mining bug had bitten him again. This time he struck gold. However, it was not in the creeks that he tried panning, but back in his cabin, where he wrote a story about a jumping frog. The story was called

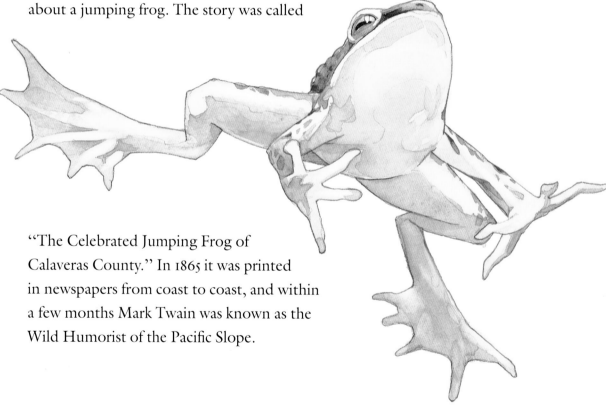

"The Celebrated Jumping Frog of Calaveras County." In 1865 it was printed in newspapers from coast to coast, and within a few months Mark Twain was known as the Wild Humorist of the Pacific Slope.

Another newspaper persuaded him to go to the Sandwich Islands, which was the name for Hawaii in those days. His assignment was to write a series of articles and stories about these lush and exotic islands. He did, and when he returned to San Francisco, he gave his first public lecture. He made his own poster, which read: DOORS OPEN AT 7 O'CLOCK. THE TROUBLE TO BEGIN AT 8 O'CLOCK. The times were the only accurate items on the poster—the rest of the information stretched the truth, manipulated all sorts of facts, and suggested absurd notions.

It was fame, not trouble, that began for Mark Twain at eight o'clock. He was thirty years old.

It would only be stretching the truth a little to say that Samuel Clemens had one of the longest childhoods in history. It lasted from the time Halley's comet streaked across the sky until Sam became Mark Twain the world-famous author.

He played hard, fought for every underdog, never stopped dreaming of buried treasure, learned to pilot a steamship from St. Louis to New Orleans, discovered war is stupid and politicians often more so. When fame found the boy who had become Mark Twain, he had to grow up fast. He did. He became celebrated as the country's wildest storyteller. He wrote many books and short stories, and like all good writers, he wrote mostly about what he knew best.

What Mark Twain knew best was being a boy on a river. He would often end his stories before the children grew up, for as he wrote on the last page of *The Adventures of Tom Sawyer:*

So endeth this chronicle. It being strictly a history of a boy, *it must stop here; the story could not go much further without becoming the history of a* man.

The comet returns

When one writes a novel about grown people, he knows exactly where to stop—that is, with a marriage; but when he writes of juveniles, he must stop where he best can.

—from THE ADVENTURES OF TOM SAWYER

IN 1870 Samuel Clemens married Olivia Langdon. They settled in Hartford, Connecticut, and had three daughters. It was after his marriage that he went on to write his classic books *The Adventures of Tom Sawyer* (1876), *The Prince and the Pauper* (1882), *Life on the Mississippi* (1883), and in 1885, his most famous novel, *Adventures of Huckleberry Finn*.

Mark Twain never claimed to be anything more than a storyteller. "I have not professionally dealt in truth. Many when they come to die spent all the truth that was in them, and enter the next world as paupers. I have saved up enough to make an astonishment there."

On April 20, 1910, Halley's comet appeared once again in the night sky. Samuel Clemens—and Mark Twain—died the next day.

BOOKS ABOUT MARK TWAIN

Allen, Jerry. *The Adventures of Mark Twain.* Boston: Little, Brown
    and Company, 1954.

Lennon, Nigey. *The Sagebrush Bohemian: Mark Twain in California.*
    New York: Paragon House, 1990.

Meltzer, Milton. *Mark Twain Himself.* Avenel, New Jersey:
    Wings Books, 1993.

Neider, Charles, ed. *The Autobiography of Mark Twain.* New York:
    Harper & Brothers, 1959.

Paine, Albert Bigelow. *Mark Twain: A Biography.*
    New York: Harper & Brothers, 1912.

Sanborn, Margaret. *Mark Twain: The Bachelor Years.* New York:
    Doubleday, 1990.

Welland, Dennis. *The Life and Times of Mark Twain.* New York:
    Crescent Books, 1991.

SELECT BOOKS BY MARK TWAIN

*The Celebrated Jumping Frog of Calaveras County, and Other
    Sketches,* 1867

The Innocents Abroad, 1869

Roughing It, 1872

The Adventures of Tom Sawyer, 1876

The Prince and the Pauper: A Tale for Young People of All Ages, 1882

Life on the Mississippi, 1883

Adventures of Huckleberry Finn, 1885

A Connecticut Yankee in King Arthur's Court, 1889

Chapters from My Autobiography, 1906

The paintings in this book were done in transparent
watercolor on paper handmade by Simon Green of the
Barcham Green mills in Maidstone, Kent, Great Britain.
The hand-lettering is by Judythe Sieck.
The text type was set in Galliard by Thompson Type, San Diego, California.
Color separations by Bright Arts, Ltd., Singapore
Printed and bound by Tien Wah Press, Singapore
This book was printed on totally chlorine-free Nymolla Matte Art paper.
Production supervision by Stanley Redfern and Pascha Gerlinger
Designed by Barry Moser and Camilla Filancia